Scheherazade Cat
The Story of a War Hero

WRITTEN BY Stephanie C. Fox

ILLUSTRATED BY Milena Radeva

Copyright © January 2016

Stephanie C. Fox

All rights reserved.

ISBN: 978-0-692-97338-7

THIS TRUE STORY IS DEDICATED TO
SCHEHERAZADE, A WONDERFUL CAT,
A GREAT LISTENER, AND THE CONSTANT
AMIABLE COMPANION OF THE AUTHOR
AND HER HUSBAND.

Bloomfield, Connecticut

Friday, June 24, 2005 　　　　　　　　　　　　　LOCAL

Kuwaiti cat saves soldiers from bombs

By Velina Nacheva

Born during the Iraqi occupation in 1991, a calico cat called Scheherazade saved the life of at least one American soldier during a recovery mission on Failaka Island. David Haines, who served as a US army chemical warfare officer during Operation Desert Storm spotted the cat playing with a small explosive device while walking through the island with some of his comrades in 1991. "Seeing her at that particular time and place saved at least one of us from death or serious injury. Although the entire unit might have walked through the area, none stepped on any live ordinance thanks to her," said Haines.

Talking about the nature and type of mines found, Haines explains that most of the individual munitions released by a cluster bomb explode on impact with the ground. However, a large number of them fail to detonate and may subsequently blow up if disturbed. "Thus, the area under the boot of one of these weaponrs becomes a kind of minefield," he said.

They are large enough to see and avoid in good light, but during periods of limited visibility, they become extremely dangerous - particularly when partly obscured by drifting sand. "As I recall, we were moving through the area during a time when the prevailing wind was from the Burgan Fields, which were still on fire," he said with a detailed and almost photographic memory of that particular time. Visibility was very bad and compounded by blowing dust. I didn't see the cat until we were almost upon her and saw her batting at a small munition (probably British, French or Russian manufacture). He then noticed that United States cluster bomblets, which have a distinctive cylindrical shape, were everywhere and figured the group were in the middle of a burst area. "We very gingerly retraced our steps and nobody got hurt," he said concluding that later, during their after-action review they decided that the cat was good luck and ought to be recruited.

Haines' unit adopted the cat as their good luck charm. "The cat did a real service and all the guys in my unit love her," Haines said. When asked if he still thinks Scheherazade is his lucky charm, "Scheherazade is the love of our (his wife and his) life.

At the age of 14 she is still lively, has a great sense of humour and talks a great deal. "She's polite to guests but reserves her devotion for my wife and me," Haines says humorously and hurries to explain that his family are equally devoted to her.

However at the moment Haines is extremely concerned by a severe dental problem that Scheherazade has developed during their last tour of duty in Kuwait. "Fortunately she's receiving expert care, courtesy of The Last Post, an organisation in Falls Village, Connecticut that has done enormously valuable work in support of animal welfare internationally," he said. Haines explained that their director, Jeanne Toomey, has arranged for Scheherazade to be treated at the Sand Road Animal Hospital, a small facility that is one of the best of its kind in the United States. He said "we're confident that she's in good hands."

Scheherazade was named after the lady in the Arabian Nights who tells endless tales in a bid to keep her life. "If she could talk Sherry (her nick name) would have numerous stories to tell. Sherry came solely on her lucky amulet was supposedly born in Failaka, the 2,300 year old ruins left by Alexander the Great, when the island still carried the name Ikaros, which according to Haines "seems to have a mystical significance to many Kuwaitis."

Haines says this story is partly sentimental to him. "I would very much like her story to be known by the US expat community in Kuwait and the Gulf States. I'm hoping this will elicit Gulf War vets who are among this audience to make public other stories of how animals did noteworthy deeds during the recent military conflicts."

"Our much loved genuine war hero Sherry" today lives with Haines and his family in the United States after having been used for target practice by the Iraqi military on the island full of active ammunitions.

On the topic of Kuwait and their pets Haines has made his observation. "Kuwait, generally speaking, is not a cat friendly place," he said elaborating that part of this has to do with a cultural tradition which is less tolerant of animals as human companions than that of America and Europe. According to him another factor contributing to what seems to be a generally antifeline attitude in Kuwait is "the country's large population of feral cats who are generally filthy, bedraggled and hostile to humans."

This aside, in all the years Haines has lived in Kuwait he has never seen a live rat, suggesting that an unappealing as the native cats may appear they're probably keeping what would otherwise be a serious rodent population under control.

Prevailing attitudes notwithstanding, he has nevertheless occasionally made the acquaintance of cat loving Kuwaitis. Among this group he mentions of Dr Farida Al-Muslla, director of the Diagnostic Laboratory Centre of the Public Authority for Agricultural Affairs and Fisheries who "keeps six cats of her own and seems to have boundless love for the entire species."

Also on the list of Kuwaitis who deserve honourable mention in the "Feline Hall of Fame is our good friend" professor Al Al-Kazemi, PhD of Kuwait University's Department of Public Administration. "All in all he is no means a cat lover. Quite the opposite, he admits to an irrational terror of the creatures as a result of a traumatic experience he had with one as a small child," Haines said. "Despite this, he has effectively become Scheherazade's godfather," Haines said and added "when she became ill, he devoted an enormous amount of his personal time and resources to make sure she got the best care available in Kuwait and always asks about her health and well being.

"Ali is an intrinsically good person and even if he doesn't personally like cats, our cat certainly likes him and we've come to consider him, his wife and children as members of our own family.

Scheherazade's story is not just a family story. There is a veteran's group and animal medical center here in New York who have taken an interest in her, which soon will also be part of a book about animals in the military or involved in military operations he's wife is writing. "So we're hoping to get other stories that can be included in the book," he concluded.

Article about Scheherazade in *The Kuwait Times*, an English language newspaper in Kuwait, June 2005.

A small calico kitten played among the ancient ruins of a town built thousands of years before she was born. Like the other cats in her country, she was small and wiry, and when she spoke, she let out a loud, plaintive, wail of a meow.

Her home, an island called Failaka, was hot, dry and dusty, like all the lands around it. Her ancestors were seafaring cats who had killed rats on ships. For this valuable service, the people on Failaka Island had treated the cats with kindness.

The Story of a War Hero

For over five thousand years, mighty empires had occupied this island on the Arabian Gulf, and then lost it during great battles.

Over many centuries, as wars raged throughout the region with the same savagery as the great sandstorms that blew in from the deserts to the west, a village on this island continued to exist. Its inhabitants became tough and wily experts at survival in a harsh environment.

THE STORY OF A WAR HERO

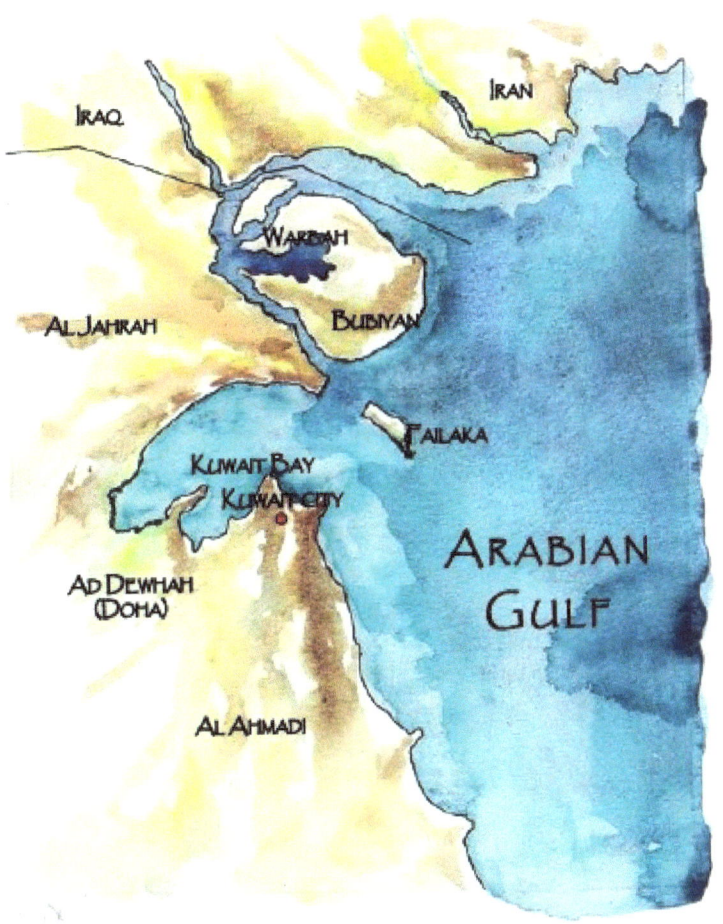

Thanks to the abundant population of fish and shrimp and oysters in the surrounding waters, Failaka Island became the home of a small fishing community.

Among the many different peoples who came to live on the island were ancient Greek pioneers, sent by Alexander the Great. They built a beautiful stone temple dedicated to their hunting goddess, Artemis.

The temple remained as a famous landmark long after the Greeks were gone. It had fallen into ruins by the time that the Kuwaitis, an Arab people, settled into the town nearby, and had become a popular archaeological site for tourists.

It was in the ruins of this temple that the little calico kitten was born.

The Story of a War Hero

During the most recent three centuries, a small settlement of Kuwaiti people became established on Failaka Island. They built homes and mosques, a souq – their word for market – and one small building called a diwaniya for men to meet and exchange news. Along the shores, they crafted and maintained their fishing nets.

That was how they earned their living: they fished, using boats called dhows, and handmade nets that were both cast overboard and set standing on the island's shoreline.

The Story of a War Hero

The government of Kuwait recognized the ancient temple as a historical treasure and began to dig out the ruins. Over a period of several years, the houses of the old Greek town and its beautiful temple were gradually uncovered, bringing the ancient history of Kuwait into the daylight after more than 2,000 years.

People from the mainland and foreign countries even came to the island to dig in the ancient ruins in search of information about the past civilizations of Failaka. Eventually, the Kuwaitis decided to set up a museum near the ruins so that citizens and visitors could appreciate the long and fascinating history of the region.

The Story of a War Hero

The Kuwaiti people had lived quite happily in their village on this island for almost three hundred years. Then one day, everything changed.

Fierce, cruel invaders came from a northern country called Iraq. They ordered all of the people off of the island.

Most people were so afraid that they left immediately, but others refused to leave their only home, and the invaders killed them.

The Iraqis then destroyed the fishing village, firing their machine guns randomly at anything that moved, including the island's cats.

The cats that had lived with the Kuwaiti people on the island were terrified of the invaders. They hid, running furtively from place to place as they searched for food, while the invaders shot at them for fun. It was a terrible time.

After several months, the invaders were driven out of Kuwait and off of Failaka Island. Soldiers from some other, faraway lands flew overhead, putting various explosive devices around the shore and all over the island.

Before the Iraqis left Kuwait, however, they destroyed everything of value that they could not steal. Black smoke from oil fires on the mainland plumed across Kuwait Bay and over Failaka Island, darkening the sky. These fires burned for months, giving the air a terrible smell, even though it came from miles away.

The Story of a War Hero

It was during this terrible time that the little calico kitten was born.

The kitten did not know any people who were kind to animals in the first few months of her life. All she knew about people was that they liked to hurt cats.

She spent her time with her mother, living among other cats in the ancient ruins. Her mother nursed her for a few months, allowing her to drink her milk, and then taught her how to hunt the few mice that lived on the island.

The Story of a War Hero

The kitten got used to the protection of her mother, and was glad to be able to run to her whenever the cats heard gunfire.

One day, the kitten's mother caught a small mouse, and refused to share it with her. The kitten was stunned. Her mother turned on her, hissing and snarling, and chased her away.

The Story of a War Hero

Sad and confused, the kitten ran off, searching for food elsewhere. After a full day during which she endured intense hunger, she heard a faint scuffling sound behind some mud-bricks – a mouse! Hopeful and excited, she crouched behind the rocks and waited, whiskers and haunches twitching in anticipation.

After several minutes of waiting, the mouse appeared. It was small, but so was the kitten. She pounced on it, claws splayed and teeth bared, killing it quickly. She picked it up with her teeth and trotted off with the tiny corpse to enjoy her meal.

The Story of a War Hero

Unfortunately, she had not gone far before she heard another, much larger, cat running towards her. The tomcat sprung on top of her and hit her as hard as he could, knocking the dead mouse out of her jaws.

The kitten knew enough not to argue with him or to attempt to keep her hard-won catch, hungry as she was. She had seen other huge tomcats kill kittens her size before. She ran away from him as fast as she could.

It was a miserable, hungry existence for the little kitten after that. She learned to keep entirely to herself, staying completely out of the sight of all of the other cats on the island, lest they steal other food from her. There was precious little for any of them to eat, and water was very scarce as well.

Somehow, the kitten managed to find enough food to stay alive, subsisting on insects and an occasional mouse that she managed to keep. She hid, avoiding gunshots from the invaders who had ruined the island. All the while, the sky overhead was black and the air foul with the stench of burning oil from the mainland.

The Story of a War Hero

One night she awoke to the crash of thunder. All around her there were flashes of light, and high in the sky she heard shrieking. Terrified, she ran into the lowest part of the ruins. The horrible noises continued the entire night, and the kitten stayed hidden.

After many hours, silence returned and the kitten cautiously emerged from the temple. What she saw was amazing. Large and small fires burned in several places and the tents of the Iraqi camp were gone. Down the small hill on which the temple was perched, she saw some Iraqis lying like broken dolls covered with blood.

The kitten was amazed. What could have happened to kill these powerful and frightening invaders?

The Story of a War Hero

Over the next few days, other people appeared. Like the Iraqis, they were soldiers who carried guns. But they did not shoot at the cats. Instead, they left them alone.

There was a new danger, however. Before coming to the island, they had to put some frightening things all over the ground in order to make the invaders go away.

The cats were almost as terrified of these things as they were of the invaders. The things were small, the same color as the desert sand, and they often exploded when touched, even if only slightly. After a few cats died from touching them, the ones who saw them die avoided these things.

The Story of a War Hero

The new soldiers were mostly from two countries called France and the United States. They came to clean up the island. The French soldiers removed the terrible dust-colored things, but very slowly and carefully. The soldiers from the United States, called Americans, removed other things left behind by the Iraqi invaders.

This took some time, and after being shot at by the Iraqis, the cats were slow to trust these newcomers. They stayed out of sight, listening and watching what went on, but soon there wasn't enough food for the cats to hunt.

The Story of a War Hero

The younger cats were more trusting of the new soldiers than the older ones, and the calico kitten had not seen the damage caused by the small explosive devices. All she knew was that she wanted food, she was lonely, and she was bored.

She came out of hiding and walked around whenever things got quiet on the island. She looked, often without success, for things to hunt and kill and eat.

The other cats had all attacked her, often stealing what little food she had been able to find. The kitten was left to her own resources to survive.

The Story of a War Hero

She walked cautiously out across the island one morning, keeping a sharp watch for signs of motion around her that could mean a mouse for dinner, or a threat to her safety from other animals or humans on the island. A small, round, dust-colored object caught her attention.

The kitten trotted over to it and swatted it. It rolled a little way away, and stopped. She raced over to it and swatted it again. It rolled off to the side, and she chased it. This was fun!

It wasn't as good as finding live prey to chase, kill and eat, but it was something, and something was better than nothing. She swatted at it and batted the round thing around some more.

The Story of a War Hero

This went on for several minutes, until she heard a loud shout: "HALT!"

The kitten stopped in mid-leap, frozen in surprise and fear. A tall soldier was standing over her, looking at her with wide blue-green eyes. He had a small gun at his side, and the soldiers he was leading had rifles.

The older cats had always chased her away from the soldiers, and now here she was, stupidly staring up at him, as close to him as she used to sit to her mother. He wasn't alone, either. He was leading a whole group of other soldiers, and they all had weapons just like his.

The Story of a War Hero

To the kitten's great surprise, the soldier did not make a move towards his weapon. He did not bother her at all.

Instead, he turned around, being careful not to move his feet while peering anxiously at the ground all around them.

He also looked up at the other soldiers. They all pointed at the kitten's toy and spoke in short, fearful sentences.

Instead of hurting or bothering the kitten, the soldiers did something even stranger than peering fearfully at the ground. They walked backwards, trying to step in their own footprints, staring into the sand and dust around them as they did so.

Soon they were gone, back the way they had come from.

The Story of a War Hero

The kitten didn't know what to make of this. What was wrong with this little ball? It didn't do anything; it just rolled around on the ground.

Bewildered and hungry, she wandered off, confused about what had just happened.

The soldier's eyes were what she remembered most about the encounter. The soldier looked at her with wide, staring, blue-green eyes. He had looked angry.

But he hadn't touched her – he just went away with the other soldiers.

The Story of a War Hero

The next day, the kitten was still hungry. She was so stunned by both the closeness of her encounter with the soldier and the expression in his eyes that she didn't want to touch that small round thing again.

She wandered across the island, feeling hungrier and lonelier than ever. The kitten sniffed the air and the ground for food again.

Just as she was feeling weak, dizzy, and sick to her stomach, dragging her feet unsteadily, she smelled something wonderful: food!

The Story of a War Hero

Other cats smelled it, too. Soon there were lots of starved, wiry-looking cats of various sizes running in the same direction as the kitten.

They were so hungry that they didn't notice that they were running towards the soldiers.

These were the same soldiers that the kitten had met the day before. They were sitting quietly outside some tents, resting and watching the cats. They stared steadily at the cats, but their eyes were not as widely open as those of the blue-green-eyed soldier's had been the day before.

Perhaps they were not angry today. The kitten decided not to worry about that – she was too hungry to care. She ran forward, towards the smell of the food.

The Story of a War Hero

There it was, a bit of dried, brown meat just lying on the desert ground. There were many, many more of these bits of dried food, and cats were finding and grabbing and eating them up.

The kitten grabbed one and hungrily began devouring it as fast as she could.

As she did so, a pair of hands enclosed her around the shoulders and lifted her up from behind.

"Got it sir!" shouted the soldier who had grabbed her.

The kitten couldn't believe what was happening to her. The soldier was carrying her across the sand toward the leader of his group, the one with the blue-green eyes who had stopped in front of her the day before. His eyes were not as wide as they had been the day before.

The kitten found herself passed to this soldier, who held her right up in front of him and smiled. "Cat!" he said, and stared intently at the little black-and-orange-and-white kitten. She stared right back.

"Cat!" he repeated, "You saved us from those little bombs! We almost walked into them!"

He wasn't angry at all, she realized. He liked her!

The Story of a War Hero

The soldier promptly gave the kitten a dish of water and some more dried food. He wanted her to stay with him!

That was fine with the kitten. She was tired of being lonely and hungry and of searching for food. She let the soldier stroke her fur and talk to her.

She liked him.

She followed the soldier into his tent and looked around.

He sat on one of the cots, and she leaped up next to him and sat down, looking down at the sand and around at the inside of the structure.

Then she curled up and went to sleep.

The Story of a War Hero

When the kitten woke up, she looked around and remembered what had happened. The soldiers were sharing what they had with her. She trusted them.

Feeling safe, she leaped down from the cot and walked around inside the tent, sniffing at the rolled up blankets, and patting the other items with her paws.

The kitten heard the sounds of the soldiers in their camp as she paced around the tent.

Suddenly, one side of the tent was pulled back and her soldier came in with a man who was not a soldier. He was a Kuwaiti citizen, and he commanded a military ship full of sailors.

The navy captain told the kitten's soldier about an Arabian woman who had one thousand stories – stories which, when told, saved lives. Her name was Scheherazade.

The Story of a War Hero

The kitten had a name now, a human being of her own, and all of the food, water, companionship and amusement she could wish for.

Scheherazade Cat was a war hero who had earned her place as a cat with a home and a human companion of her very own.

The Story of a War Hero

58

The U.S. Army officer who had adopted her, 1st Lieutenant David D. Haines, was heartbroken to learn that it would not be possible to bring his loyal cat with him by military transport on his redeployment to America.

With both sadness and gratitude, he left Scheherazade with his friend, the Kuwait Navy captain who had suggested her name.

The Story of a War Hero

Scheherazade thoroughly enjoyed her summer as the ship's cat, with all of the mice she could kill and no other cats to challenge her right to keep them. The sailors aboard all knew her story, so they treated her with honor and made sure that she had other good food to eat as well.

The Story of a War Hero

When the summer ended, Scheherazade got a wonderful surprise: David was back in Kuwait, but not as a soldier. He was back as a civilian scientist – and to collect his cat! At last, she could move in with him permanently.

Her life as an honored combat veteran had officially begun.

It was a better reward for saving the soldiers than winning a medal.

THE END

About the Hero

This book honors a wonderful cat who honorably served her native land in wartime and was thus awarded United States citizenship and a good life with people who loved her.

This brave veteran, who survived the Persian Gulf War behind enemy lines for the first part of her life, lost her final battle in 2005, surrendering to cancer, which the armies of Saddam Hussein and a harsh desert could not claim.

She is sadly missed and will always be remembered with great affection. The following pages pay additional respect to some of her human friends who proudly shared her wartime adventures:

Scheherazade Cat, sleeping.

About the Lieutenant

First Lieutenant David D. Haines, United States Army, was Nuclear, Biological, and Chemical Defense officer for a downtrace unit of the 82nd Airborne Division during the Persian Gulf War. Following the conflict, he was part of a special operation, commanded by General Charles Getz (U.S. Army, Retired), to identify and retrieve high-value military equipment left in Kuwait by retreating Iraqi forces. It was during the performance of a part of this mission, which Lt. Haines organized with the Kuwait Navy, that he met Scheherazade.

After leaving the Army in 1991, he earned a Ph.D. in Immunology and has devoted his career to characterization of chronic illness among populations exposed to military toxicants. In this capacity, he established the first collaborative program since 1979, between American and Iranian scientists for the study of chemical weapons effects. He is co-founder and Chief Science Officer for Essential Biotherapeutics, S.A.R.L., a Swiss-registered biotechnology corporation established to make use of findings in studies of war-linked illness for the development of novel approaches to the prevention of and therapy for serious chronic disease.

He is widely published in peer-reviewed scientific literature and is currently director of TRINITY, a program focused on cellular senescence, designed to utilize adaptive responses to oxidative stress in ways with potential for lifespan extension. Dr. Haines is currently employed as a pharmaceutical researcher at the Faculty of Pharmacy, Department of Pharmacology, University of Debrecen, in Debrecen, Hungary. He is married to the author of this book.

Lieutenant Haines in wardroom of the warship *Istiqlal*, May 1991.

About the Captain

Captain Marc Garcia, United States Army, was a Military Police & Special Operations Forces (Civil Affairs) officer who served with Lieutenant Haines in the equipment collection operation. During this operation, Captain Garcia used his experience as a U.S. State Department security specialist to build a network of military and private sector support for the equipment recovery mission. Captain Garcia remained in the Army following the war and retired as a full Colonel in 2013.

Captain Marc Garcia

Captain Marc Garcia.

About the Major

As **Major Frank J. LaBuda,** United States Army, he was assigned to the 22nd Support COSCOM during the Persian Gulf War, charged with providing logistical support to units in the field. His specialty was military prosecution and war crimes investigation.

After the war, Major LaBuda worked with Lieutenant Haines to collect information that was later used by investigators at the University of Connecticut, for research into health effects of wartime chemical exposure.

Following his return to the United States, Major LaBuda was appointed as a New York State Supreme Court Judge. He remained in the Army as a reserve officer, and retired as a colonel in 2011.

Major Frank J. LaBuda.

Kuwait Navy Captain Khalid Al-Kandari worked with Lieutenant Haines' team to provide Kuwaiti naval assets in support of efforts to recover abandoned equipment on Failaka Island.

These efforts included repair and restoration of the civilian ferry used by the Iraqis to resupply their garrison on the island during the occupation. Lieutenant Haines, Captain Garcia, and their Kuwaiti colleagues were eventually able to use this boat to move a large number of Iraqi armored vehicles to the mainland, where General Getz facilitated their use in ongoing Allied military operations.

Captain Khalid Al-Kandari, left, with Abdulhameed Al-Othman, right, also known as "The Ghost of Failaka".

About the Author

Stephanie C. Fox, J.D. is a historian, author, and editor. She is a graduate of William Smith College and the University of Connecticut School of Law. She runs an editing service called *QueenBeeEdit*, which caters to politicians, military officers, physicians, and scientists.

Ms. Fox has written several books on a variety of topics, including the effects of human overpopulation on the environment, Asperger's, and travel to Kuwait and Hawai'i. Her areas of interest include – but are not limited to – history, herstory, women's studies, biographies, dystopian and science fiction, environmental studies and environmental law, international relations, the economic meltdown of 2008, and cats.

Stephanie C. Fox, sitting in a traditional Kuwaiti tent, woven by the women of Al Sadu House.

About the Illustrator

Milena Radeva is a children's book illustrator living and working in Bulgaria. Milena works in the field of children's books illustration and owes her unique style to the fact that her illustrations are all hand-drawn.

She graduated in Illustration from the National Art Academy of Sofia in 2012, and she is working on her Ph.D. thesis about Bulgarian illustrations.

In 2014, Milena Radeva and her colleague, Ilia Boyarov, presented their first exhibition: *Animalia*. It features scientific illustration and sculpture, which in 2015 made a national tour in 12 cities. In 2016, Milena and Ilia will present their second exhibition, *Animalia Aves*.

Milena has illustrated more than 50 books for publishers and authors around the world, and is looking forward to many more!

Milena Radeva.

SCHEHERAZADE CAT

Scheherazade Cat
The Story of a War Hero

WRITTEN BY **Stephanie C. Fox**
ILLUSTRATED BY Milena Radeva

Article about Scheherazade in *The Register Citizen*, a Connecticut newspaper, September 2004, shortly before she accompanied Dr. Haines and his wife Stephanie, the author of this book, on a return visit to Kuwait where they lived for a year.

Scheherazade Cat, napping.

www.ingramcontent.com/pod-product-compliance
Lightning Source LLC
Chambersburg PA
CBHW042051290426
44110CB00001B/24